# Boggart

Written and illustrated
by Ros Asquith

Now listen here. The time has come to save the Saddest Man in the world.

The time has come to read a story that begins with these words:

'Now listen here. The time has come to save the Saddest Man in the world.'

So, good. Good start. You're reading that very story. Congratulate yourself. Give yourself a big pat on the back. (If you can reach your back. Try it, it's harder than it sounds.)

But slow down. You've got to open the next page slowly. Did you hear that?

# S. L. O. W. L. Y.

OK, here goes. Turn it now.

Sorry, that was too fast. When I say slowly, I mean:

# S. L. O. W. L. Y.

That's the trouble. Everything moves too fast, everyone busy, busy, busy, jumping in and out of the Internet, lolloping around like an itchy walrus, saying: 'Can't you see I'm busy? I've no time.'

Well, here's a secret.

There's plenty of time. Time is everywhere. You can't live without it. So take your time.

Otherwise how are you going to catch the Boggart of Baker Street?

And if the Boggart escapes, how are you going to save the Saddest Man in the world?

Remember, when I say slowly, I mean:

S.

    L.

        O.

           W.

              L.

                Y.

(OK, turn it.)

Too fast. Look, maybe this is the wrong book for you. Maybe you don't really enjoy reading books? Or maybe you don't care very much about the Saddest Man in the world?

Fair enough.

People are often sad and you can't help all of them.

But this story is about a kind-hearted boy (his name is Joe) who does care about such things. Joe lives alone with his granny and, oh, all right, maybe Joe has other reasons to find the Saddest Man. Kindness alone is not always enough. Maybe Joe himself is sad, too? Still, Joe definitely wants to find him.

So, if you *do* want to help Joe to catch the Boggart and save the Saddest Man, you've got to turn this page slower than grass growing.

Tell you what, to help you, think of a snail.

Then think of another snail that's slower

than the first snail. Then another that's even slower than that. OK?

(If someone is telling you to get on and read quickly, then explain the situation to them. Explain that you are out to save the Saddest Man in the world and that these things take time.)

Ready? Steady? S L O W!

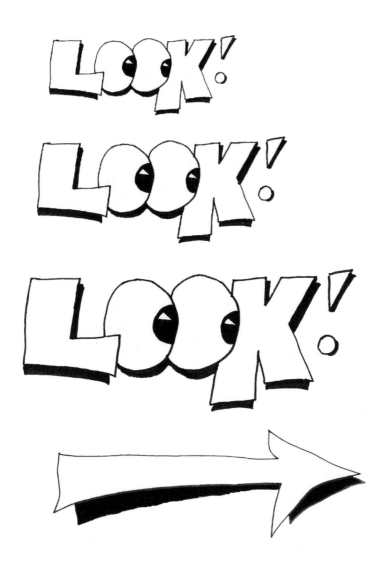

There. Over there is the Boggart!

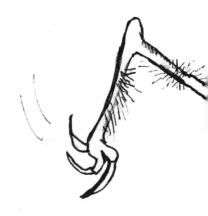

Well, there is its foot, at least. Boggarts are hard to spot.

Now you must be quicker than a plate of lightning soup.

Turn this page really *fast* to catch it.

Excellent.
Joe's inside this
story so he can't
turn any pages.
But he may need
you to help him
again, so please stay
right where you are,
just in case.

Joe remembered that
the Saddest Man's mum had told him:
'When you find a Boggart, you must ask it what
it's got to say for itself. And you must speak in a
hissing sort of voice to a Boggart.'

So Joe did.

'Now lisssssten here, Boggart, what have you
got to sssay for yoursssssself? Eh?'

'Good morning, afternoon or evening,
whatever time it is in your neck of the woods,'

replied the Boggart. 'Pray forgive me if I sound impolite, but why are you hissing like a balloon in a tizzy?'

Joe didn't expect the Boggart to have good manners. Joe thought it would be a lousy-no-good-saddest-man-stealing-burglaring Boggart.

Also, Joe saw that the Boggart was very small, roughly the size of two ants or a quarter of a caterpillar, or 408 grains of sand. So how could it help him search the world for the Saddest Man? Because the world is very big, like a lot of ants all stuck together. Or even more sand.

'Oh, why did I ever bother catching you?' said Joe.

'I dunno,' retorted the Boggart. 'Why?'

'I want to find the Saddest Man in the world,' said Joe. 'But you're no help.'

'Oh no?' said the Boggart. 'And why would that be?'

'Because you're too small,' said Joe. 'You're no bigger than a bluebottle's underpants.'

'I am too,' said the Boggart, in quite a huff. 'I'm as big as – as – a worm's pyjamas. Nearly.'

'Still, you're too small to go all round the world hunting for the Saddest Man.'

'Don't judge a book by its cover,' said the Boggart.

(Which means, if you didn't know, not just that a dull-looking dusty old book might be full of wonderful things, or even that a glossy book with colourful superheroes striding about on its cover might be a yawn. It means, you can't tell what someone is like by looking at them.)

To prove his point, the Boggart expanded to the size of a small armchair.

'You'll never find the Saddest Man without *me*,' he declared, and vanished in an explosion.

As you see, he burnt the page. Boggarts do that when they're cross – they live in a land of smoke and mirrors.

'Oh, no!' cried Joe. 'Sorry I was rude. Please come back. Please help me find the Saddest Man.'

But there was no reply, because the Boggart had vanished in a puff of smoke.

I expect you have heard that phrase, 'vanished in a puff of smoke' before. Well, this time it really happened.

Joe looked high and low.

You can look too. Try looking at the ceiling and at your feet. Try looking at the sky and even lower than your feet.

Any luck? Well Joe didn't have any luck either. Joe looked everywhere. He saw plenty of things: socks, crumbs, dead biscuits.

But no Boggart.

'Look for a sign,' came an eerie, Boggarty voice. Joe looked out of his bedroom window and saw plenty of signs.

All sorts of signs telling him what he couldn't do. But no sign of the Boggart.

*Joe sat down and sighed.*
*It can't be denied,*
*Joe felt sorry inside.*
*'Oh, Boggart,' he cried.*
*'Why must you hide?*
*I think you lied*
*and took me for a ride.*
*Oh, well. I tried.'*
*'Not very hard,'*
*the Boggart replied.*

(Why is this a poem? Boggarty magic?)

Joe saw that the Boggart, now normal Boggart-size (about like a small sheep or a large dog), had made himself comfortable under Joe's duvet and was devouring Joe's crisps, bag and all.

'Please help me,' said Joe.

'Why should I help a schnortwurggling, snooplarking, slug of a boy like you?' said the Boggart, showing his true colours.

By the way, this didn't mean he showed Joe that he was striped like a rainbow or decorated in lilac and emerald checks under his hairy chest; it meant he showed what sort of person, or Boggart, he really was. But he quickly thought better of it and said in his polite voice, 'Only joking, no offence. Let's start again, shall we? How can I be of service?'

Can you guess why the Boggart had second thoughts? Perhaps this will give you a clue.

# DAILY NEWS

## CAN YOU FIND THE SADDEST MAN AND MAKE HIM HAPPY? GENEROUS REWARD OFFERED

*'He may be sad but he's my boy and I want him back,' says Saddest Man's mum.*

'I just want to find the Saddest Man,'
sniffed Joe.

'And why might that be?'

'Because his mum is now the saddest woman
in the world and finding him would make
her happy.'

'And why, if I may ask, do you wish to make
her happy?'

But Joe went pink, then red, then scarlet, then
vermillion, then maroon (oh and some other
colourful shades that I can't be bothered to go
into), but he wouldn't say why. So there was
quite a

# looooooooooooooong

silence.

Actually, the silence lasted a whole page, so
you can take a short break from reading this
book now if you like, as the next page after this
is blank. Do whatever you want, go to the toilet,
have a sandwich, check for earwax, whatever
you fancy.

Oooh, I hope you're back, because the story's starting up again and I wouldn't want you to miss any of it.

After the looooong silence, the Boggart asked Joe: 'It wouldn't be that you were after a reward, would it?'

'What reward?' asked Joe, who didn't read newspapers.

'Nothing, nothing at all,' said the Boggart, twirling his tail charmingly and lying through his teeth.

(Sorry to keep interrupting, but that is a strange phrase, isn't it? How else can you tell a lie, except through your teeth? Unless you are writing, of course, as I am doing ... )

'So can you help?' asked Joe, gloomily.

'Well, as it happens, I can and I can't,' said the Boggart, ferreting about in his rucksack. He then drew out a scroll and waved it in front of Joe's face. Joe wrinkled his nose.

'It smells of socks.'

'*Socks*?' snarled the Boggart. 'Socks? It's made of finest green cheese, flattened paper-thin by water buffaloes. I keep it in my rucksack to save it from mice.'

Joe held his nose and peered at the scroll.

> *The search you have begun may never end.*
> *Saddest is he who never finds a friend.*
> *Man looks for happiness but, truly, what*
> *Is better than what he's already got?*
> *Behind, above, below, you look and look.*
> *The key is in the pages of this book.*
> *Round every corner you may find a clue.*
> *Door after door MAY open, just for you.*

'Forgive me for saying so, but that's not very helpful,' said Joe.

'Well, that shows how little you know,' said the Boggart, 'but even if it's not a good clue (which it is), he can only be saved if someone can make him happy. And I can't do that.'

'Why?'

'Boggarts don't know how to make anyone happy, it's not in our nature,' said the Boggart. 'But if you want to try, let's give it a go.'

Then the Boggart grabbed Joe's hand in his furry claw and they both vanished! In two puffs of smoke.

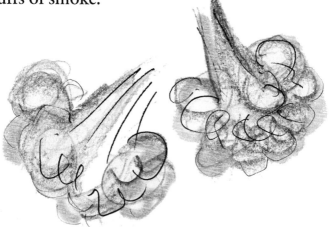

Oh dear.
Oh dear, oh dear, oh dear.

They really have vanished. Oh no. This story is getting a little out of hand.

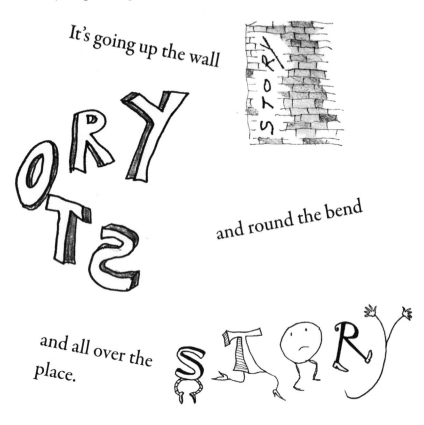

It's going up the wall

and round the bend

and all over the place.

I'm really sorry. I thought you were just going to have to help Joe. But now you are going to have to do all the work. You are going to have to find the Saddest Man *and* Joe.

Look. Fair enough. You didn't sign up for this. You just agreed to help out a bit. But now you're in it up to your neck.

Here's a selection of necks. You can choose the one which is most like yours.

Or, you can put this book right back on the shelf and get on with something useful, like daydreaming or ballet or playing football or counting the leaves on that old tree down the road. Or inventing a new word.

Honestly, I didn't mean for this to happen, I won't blame you if you

# STOP
## READING RIGHT NOW.

(You can even show your teacher this page to prove it's not your fault).

OK?

No hard feelings. But, just one little thing that might interest you before you go.

The Boggart dropped something, just as he and Joe vanished in two puffs of smoke. It looks like a scruffy old torn sheet of paper, but, in fact, it's a map – a sort of treasure mappy kind of map, in fact, with a kind of 'X marks the spot' on it.

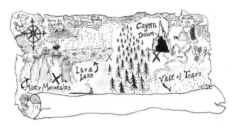

I think the Boggart will be fuming and spitting fire when he finds he's lost that map, because I expect that map shows where the Saddest Man is. I imagine that old Boggarty will be zipping back here to find that map. And if he does, I guess he might bring Joe back safely.

But then again, he might not.

And do you know, I've had a thought. I think it would be wonderful and a hundred million kinds of sweet and marvellous if you did want to use that map yourself to find the Saddest Man before the Boggart does.

You know why? I don't trust that Boggart one tiny bit. I'm pretty sure he's up to no good. Because Boggarts are famous for mischief and child-stealing and all kinds of general meanness and unworthy things. So. You can either:

# STOP
## READING RIGHT NOW
## or
## you can read the map.

If you do decide to read the map to see if you can find the Saddest Man in the world, it might get tricky. But you can change your mind and give up half way, because sometimes abandoning hard stuff is the right thing to do.

Well, are you still here?

OK, if so, take a deep breath, because when you get to the next page you are going to have to turn this book upside down, otherwise you won't understand a word.

By the way, here's the key to the map. You'll need it when you've decided where to go.

Key to map:

Cavern of Doom: go to page 34
Vale of Tears: go to page 38
Fiery Furnace: go to page 32
Misty Mountains: go to page 41
Lake of bubbling poisonous Lava: go to page 40
Very Nice Sweetshop packed full of your favourite sweeties: go to page 46

OK. Ready? Turn the page upside down and go.

# NOW.

If you're STILL stuck, try page 52.

Here be
Jelly-fish

Cavern
of
DooM

Vale of Tears

X marks ye spot

P.S. When you have looked everywhere,
go to page 50.

Well done. You turned it upside down.

Full marks. Here is the map. X marks the spot.

Ha. Typical Boggart. X marks the spot indeed! Which X?

Maybe it's time to have a little think.

1. Has the Boggart laid a trap?

2. Is he lying in wait for you (or waiting to lie to you) in the Cavern of Doom? Or the Very Nice Sweetshop? He's likely to choose the sweetshop, because baddies often trap you in nice places, wearing nice faces and smart clothes.

3. Anyway, where is the Saddest Man?

4. He's bound to be in the Vale of Tears, as that is the saddest place. Or maybe he went to the sweetshop to cheer himself up? Or he could be, well, anywhere, or nowhere.

This is tricky.

How can you choose?

But wait a minute. I've just realized you can visit all these places. If you're wrong the first time, you can always try another way. Life's like that. It gives you second chances.

Now, you can do whatever you want, but my advice is, go back to the map (remember to turn the book upside down first), close your eyes, wiggle your finger about and then stab it into the page and go to the nearest X.

Off you go.

(If you've changed your mind, don't worry, someone else is bound to have a go. They may find the Saddest Man. Don't feel too bad about it.)

If he isn't in any of those places, I guess we can just go to page 50. But I don't think we should go there *yet* because we might miss him and it might be a trap.

# The Fiery Furnace

Hey, no. Wrong choice.

This whole page is burning up! If the Saddest Man is here, he'll be toast.

And no butter.

Or jam.

Quick. Scuttle back to the map faster than a skittle.

Try again.

# The Cavern of Doom

Hmm. Dark. Deep. Doomy. Doooooooomy.
Very. Tell you what, stay outside and shout in,
nice and loud, because the Saddest Man might
be hiding at the back.

Hello?

Hello, hello, hello …

Someone answered! Did you hear?

Here, here, here …

See? Someone's inside!

Sighed, sighed, sighed …

And whoever it is, is sighing. It must be the
Saddest Man. Be careful.

Full, full, full …

He's saying the cavern's
full. Maybe there are
baddies in there. Mind
how you go.

Go, go, go …

Now wait a minute,
he's telling you to go away.
Maybe he doesn't want to
be rescued. You decide.
What do you want to
do? Go or stay?

STAY, STAY, STAY …

Now that's confusing. Oh, hang on
a minute, I don't think there's anyone
there at all. Nobody.

Body, body, body …

Don't be scared, it's not a dead body in there, either, it's just an echo. See?

See, see, see …

Honest, this cave is empty, not full.

FOOL, FOOL, FOOL …

Oh, we're getting the rudest man in the world now. If you don't believe me, try it yourself. Try shouting any old word, like *cardboard*.

Bored, bored, bored …

I'm bored too. There's nobody there. Let's go back to the map.

Still don't believe me?

Shout, very loud, a silly word:
*Carbuncle*!

Buncle, buncle, buncle …

Ah, I see you do believe me at last. I know it's sad that the Saddest Man isn't in there. I know you do want to find him, but he just isn't *there*.

Quick, back to the map.

# Vale of Tears

This is gloomy. We need an umbrella. Who made all these statues? Your face is wet, try licking your lips. Thought so.

Tastes salty, doesn't it? It's not rain.

It really *is* tears.

Maybe they are the Saddest Man's tears?

Saddest Man? Are you here? Are you sadly making statues and weeping all the while?

Come home and be safe with us.

Look. There he is!

No! It's a gorgon. Don't look in her eyes.

She'll turn you to stone!

Quick, back to the map! Again!

# The Lava Lake

Glug, glug. Double, double, toil and trouble, oozey, gooey lava bubble.

Urk. No. Keep to the top of the page. Don't fall in there.

No way could anyone survive here.

Back to the map.

Quick.

# The Misty Mountains

Goodness, *so* misty.

You can't even see your hand in front of your face.

*It's a disgrace,*
*Not a nice place.*
*A horrible space.*
*Shall we look, just in case?*

Humph. That Boggarty old poem thing is interrupting us. Now, stop and think.

Wave your hand around to see if the mist clears.

Goodness, what high mountains. And the ground is covered in ... bones. Hmm, I see a sign. Shall we read it?

Listen, I know you're brave, you wouldn't have come this far if you weren't. But if 'No one survives,' I think we can agree that the Saddest Man isn't here. But wait, here's a cave.

THESE BONES ARE THE BONES OF IDIOTS, NINCOMPOOPS, DIMWITS AND VERY SILLY PEOPLE WHO TRIED TO CLIMB THE MISTY MOUNTAINS. NO ONE SURVIVES SO GET REAL AND GET OUT.

Anybody in there? Coooeee, anyone at home?

No one.

Oh, very clever. Obviously there is someone inside. Shall we tiptoe in?

Excuse me, sorry to bother you, but we're looking for the Saddest Man in the world.

You won't find him here. No one can survive here. You won't last five minutes.

But you survived.

Yes – but I am ...

Aaaargh!

*Let's get out of here!*

Back to the map!

# A Very Nice Sweetshop

Look at all those wonderful sweets.

But wait, who are those little people?

We are the gummy goblins
Gobbling lovely sweets.
We are the fudgy fairies
Stirring fudgy treats.
We are the eating elves
Who like to stuff and stuff ourselves
Jelly beans, liquorice, chocolate candy
Any sweets that come in handy.
Especially very sweet girls and boys
Who should be at home
Playing with their toys.
Let's catch 'em and cook 'em,
They're ever so sweet,
And soon they'll be wrapped
And delicious to eat.

Oh dear, I think they mean *us*.
I thought those sweeties had rather
peculiar labels ... Quick, back
to the map.

**49**

**HAH!**

IF YOU LOOKED HERE BEFORE YOU LOOKED ANYWHERE ELSE YOU WILL BE QUITE UPSET BECAUSE THERE IS NOTHING HERE **AT ALL.**

Oh dear. The Saddest Man wasn't in any of those places.

That is a typical Boggarty trick. He has left the map on purpose for us to find, while he goes off with Joe to get the Saddest Man. Then he'll make Joe get the reward and he won't hand the Saddest Man over until he gets the money and we've been wasting precious time.

Yes, yes, I know I said that time is everywhere and there's plenty of it, but that isn't always true. Sometimes you do have to hurry.

Now get your skates on.

OK?

But hang on one second. I've just remembered a tiny thing. I think I might be wrong, but I just might be right. Did you notice some very tiny tiny writing near the corner of the map? I don't think we paid it any attention, because it was mirror writing and it was very small. Maybe that was the clue. Let's have one more look, shall we?

If you're still stuck, try page 52.

If you're still stuck, try page 52.

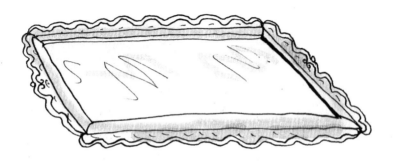

Hah! This is where the real clues start.
Follow the maze, to the Wise Old Woman.

Congratulations! You saved that scary bog-slimy creature! You kindly carried him up the ladder and you found the Wise Old Woman.

(Don't worry if her house looks a bit ramshackle, the houses of the wisest people often look rather like that. And now you know that WOW stands for Wise Old Woman.)

The Wise Old Woman scrubbed the bog-slimy creature with hot water and soap. Guess what? He was Joe!

He'd been dropped in the bog by the Boggart, who got bored with him when he couldn't find the Saddest Man. Boggarts are like that.

'I had no idea you were stuck in the bog. I should've known when I saw that wicked old Boggart,' exclaimed the Wise Old Woman.

'You saw him?'

'Yes. I got rid of him soon enough. I told him that if he stayed away while the holly was green, he'd have all his heart's desires later.'

'But holly's always green,' said Joe.

'Yes,' cackled the Wise Old Woman. 'And Boggarts is always stupid.'

'Thank you, but can you tell us where the Saddest Man is?' said Joe.

'Somewhere behind that door. Have a muffin before you go.'

It's a delightful idea, but I don't think we have time just now.

I don't know about you, but I simply can't *wait* to find the Saddest Man.

A notice like that isn't going to keep me out. You can come too, if you like.

So much for going through that door. Now look. Another load of doors. How on Earth can we choose one to go through?

Let's look at this upside down writing.
Turn the page around to read it.

*Go to page 21 and read the first word of each line on the scroll.*

OK, let's go to page 21, quicker than parsnips.

Well. He is obviously behind the round door. That's what it said, so that's where he is.

'Saddest Man, are you in there?'

Try again.

'Saddest Man, are you in there?'

Try again.

'Saddest Man, are you in there?'

'Go away.'

'Please come out to play.'

'Boo, hoo, hoo, go away.'

'Why are you so sad, Saddest Man?'

'Boo, hoo, hoo, oh, oh, oh, because I have no friends.'

'LOTS of people have no friends. Joe here has no friends either. He's quite sad, too, but he doesn't hide away all the time crying. You'll never make any friends like that.'

'Boo, hoo, hoo. Oh, oh, oh, woe is me, oh, oh oh oh. Boo hoo ...'

This is getting boring. I think we should just go inside, don't you? We've come a long way. I know it's not polite to barge in, but let's do it anyway.

Oh dear, he's so sad.

Look at him wailing and crying and weeping and moaning and gnashing his sad little teeth and stretching his sad, big eyes.

We have found the Saddest Man *at last*, but how can we make him happy?

He's sadder than sad.

Joe looks sad too.

'He's not looking at me, he doesn't seem to know I'm here,' said Joe. 'But wait, I think I know what to do. Turn the page upside down.'

OK, I'll try anything once.

Are you ready?

Turn the page upside down on the count of three.

one,

two,

THREE.

It worked! The Saddest Man saw Joe! And guess what he said?

So Joe and the Saddest Man went home
arm in arm. And the Saddest Man's mum (who
was Joe's granny, as I expect you've guessed),
was very happy indeed.

Is this the end of the story or the beginning
of the end? Or the end of the beginning?

There's never really an ending, only a place
where the story stops. For now.

You might like to think about what happened before you opened this book. Maybe the Saddest Man was sad because Joe's mum had run away and he'd gone off to find her, leaving Joe with his granny? Or perhaps he had been kidnapped (or man-napped) by the Boggart?

And what do you think happens next?

Now that the Saddest Man isn't sad any more there must be another man somewhere who is now the Saddest Man in the world, mustn't there? Life's like that.

But look, you've done very well.

Very well indeed.

You've made *this* Saddest Man happy. You deserve a doughnut. With icing. And sprinkles.

Bye for now.

(Pssst! Watch out for Boggarts.)

## About the author

I've spent the last twenty years making jokes, sometimes as cartoons in newspapers, but often in books like *Letters from an Alien Schoolboy* (shortlisted for the Roald Dahl funny Prize) or *It's Not Fairy*, about a fairy who eats parents (oh, and kids) if they whinge too much.

I liked the idea of making a funny book about someone really sad, but then the Boggart turned up, all whiskery and whirry, snorting and galumphing about. Can you help to sort him out and save the Saddest Man? That would make me a very happy writer.